BOOK ANALYSIS

By Jim Hilton

The Waves

BY VIRGINIA WOOLF

VIRGINIA WOOLF

ENGLISH WRITER

- **Born in London in 1882.**
- **Died in Rodmell (United Kingdom) in 1941.**
- **Notable works:**
  - *Jacob's Room* (1922), novel
  - *Mrs Dalloway* (1925), novel
  - *To the Lighthouse* (1927), novel

Virginia Woolf was one of the most important Modernist authors of the 20th century and a pioneer in the use of many experimental prose devices. She was part of the Bloomsbury group, an artistic and literary group of intellectuals and bohemians who shared ideas about philosophy and the arts and rejected traditional habits. Woolf was also a prominent women's rights advocate and the founder of the Hogarth Press, through which she published most of her works.

During her literary career, her prose continuously evolved towards more experimental storytelling and narrative devices. For instance, she was a trailblazer in the use of the stream of consciousness technique (a literary device that strives to capture the multitude of thoughts that pass through a character's mind as part of a non-linear narrative).

Her life and work were affected by her sporadic mental breakdowns: she was institutionalised and attempted suicide on multiple occasions during her lifetime. At the age of 59, having fallen into another bout of depression and feeling anxious about the onset of World War II, she drowned herself in the river Ouse, near Monk's House, her home in Sussex (United Kingdom).

THE WAVES

WOOLF'S HIGH MODERNIST EVOCATION OF TIME'S EFFECTS ON SIX FRIENDS

- **Genre:** poetic prose, Modernist fiction
- **Reference edition:** Woolf, V. (2006) *The Waves*. London: Penguin.
- **1st edition:** 1931
- **Themes:** time, death, nature, love, aging, reality and illusion

First published by the Hogarth Press in 1931, *The Waves* was Virginia's Woolf's seventh novel, and it is widely regarded as her most experimental. Its rapturous and fragmentary style have made it largely resistant to adaptation; however, in 2006 it was adapted for the stage in a production directed by Katie Mitchell (British theatre director, born in 1964) which played at the National Theatre.

The Waves traces the intertwining lives of six friends, from childhood and heady adolescence through to middle and old age. Each chapter opens with an italicised descriptive passage of waves breaking against the shore, as the sun rises, and finally sets towards the end of the novel. The chapters themselves are told through the voices of the six friends: Bernard, Susan, Louis, Rhoda, Neville and Jinny. Their voices do not, however, resemble the language of ordinary speech, nor any typical style of first-person narration. Rather, they speak in long rhapsodic soliloquies which seem addressed not so much to the reader as to the universe. They speak with all the vast poetic clarity of Woolf's extraordinary imagination, and yet remain distinct personalities with their own trajectories. We move with them through life, through school, university, careers and marriage, bearing witness to their fears and longings, and to their reverence for each other, and the union of friendship which continues to draw them together. Woolf's enchanting and at times highly difficult novel remains a masterpiece of English literature and a bold experiment in Modernist fiction.

SUMMARY

Each chapter begins with a descriptive passage in italics, describing the motion of the waves on a beach, and the effect of the sunlight as it advances at dawn, moves across the sky, and finally sets towards the end of the novel.

In the first chapter, Bernard, Susan, Louis, Rhoda, Neville and Jinny are children at school together. Susan spots Jinny kissing Louis, which angers her. She runs off crying and is comforted by Bernard, who is instinctively sympathetic and seeks to allay Susan's feelings by being amusing.

In the second chapter, the six are now adolescents and have all been sent off to boarding schools. The girls each crave their freedom, but for different reasons: Jinny feels ready for society and its attendant excitements, while Susan suffocates within the strictures of school authority and longs for the open sky and empty fields. Bernard, Neville and Louis meanwhile have all become friends with Percival, who is a greatly respected boy at their school. Bernard flourishes in the jocular atmosphere of boyhood, while Neville finds the overbearing authority of the school stultifying and repugnant.

The third chapter finds Bernard and Neville at university. Neville's affection for Percival has by this time become romantic in nature, and his love for him fuels his search for poetic beauty. Bernard meanwhile imagines himself as a young Byron, but is beginning to struggle with the process of translating his love of language into written words, and he struggles to write a love letter to an unnamed sweetheart. Louis has got a job at a shipping firm, but is still plagued by insecurity as well as loftier and more poetic ambitions. Susan is back in the countryside and restored to her rightful element, while Jinny and Rhoda attend the same party in London. Jinny is set free among people, finding herself wanted and appreciated, while Rhoda feels the forlorn outsider.

The fourth chapter opens a few years later. Neville is in a restaurant anxiously awaiting the arrival of Percival. The six of them are throwing a lunch party to mark Percival's departure to India to serve in the colonial government, and one by one the other five of them slowly arrive. Susan, rugged and rural, feels threatened by the highly feminine and cosmopolitan appearance of Jinny, while Rhoda feels uneasy and invisible. The atmosphere is lightened considerably by Percival's arrival, and Bernard informs everyone that he is engaged to be married.

The fifth chapter takes place not too long after the fourth. Bernard's son has just been born, but they have also all just received news that Percival has been thrown from his horse and killed in India. Neville is heartbroken, while Bernard is torn between joy for his son and grief for his friend. He bitterly remembers an occasion when Percival asked him "to go to Hampton Court" and Bernard "refused" (p. 119). Taking a rare moment of solitude, Bernard goes to the National Gallery to look at paintings, while Rhoda goes to watch an opera.

In the sixth chapter we learn that Rhoda and Louis have become lovers. Louis is by now a respectable figure in his shipping company, and yet his imagination is still restless. Jinny continues to enjoy London's party lifestyle, while Susan, on her farm, is now a mother. She reflects on her life, which is on one hand richer and more complete, while on the other, it is squeezed ever more tightly in a vice.

By the seventh chapter, all six characters have now entered middle age. Bernard takes a re-flective break in Rome, over which he begins to come to terms with all the things he will never do or see. Neville continues to write poetry and move between lovers, while Jinny realises with sadness that she is no longer young – her powers of attraction are fading and she must adjust to a different pace of life. Rhoda meanwhile has left England and Louis for Spain and, while climbing a hill, she has a clifftop vision.

In the eighth chapter the six are meeting together for dinner at Hampton Court. It takes time for them to warm up around each other, and each of their appearances seems to challenge the choices made by each of the others. Neville and Susan find themselves in unspoken conflict, as the divergence of their lives seems overt and weighted. Finally, the mist clears and the six of them recover that sense of union again. They all take a walk through the woods, and Louis and Rhoda take a small moment to themselves in which they can acknowledge the erstwhile connection between them, before the others re-join them and the moments passes.

The final chapter is told entirely by Bernard, who speaks as if to a vague acquaintance he has bumped into while the two of them have dinner. Now an old man, Bernard attempts to sum up his life, and goes over much of the action of the novel. It is here we learn that Rhoda has killed herself in the intervening time since the previous chapter. Bernard remains unsure about the soundness of his life's project, but finally – after his companion leaves – he is comfortable and happy being alone.

CHARACTER STUDY

BERNARD

Bernard is the character we spend most time with in the novel, and the final chapter is all his, as he tells his life story to a loose acquaintance over dinner. Bernard is the vehicle for Woolf's worldly interests: he is the storyteller, constantly weaving phrases and noting them down in a little book. From childhood he knows that his power is in language, but it is an effusive and an intrinsically social power – one which buoys him up and makes him comfortable in the company of servants and of gentlemen, but which seems to evaporate and elude him as soon as he is alone. Try as he might, he cannot summon up all his neat phrases into the one great final phrase for which is constantly searching. He is a tireless observer of human life and a crafter of stories, and yet again, he cannot seem to draw together the ultimate story which takes account of the world's infinite variety. His story-telling is an aspect of his performative nature, and like most performative people, he thrives in company. He lives off the gaiety of life, appreciating laughter and singing, and of course the good reception of his wit by others – on whom he knows he depends for his sense of self.

SUSAN

Susan is the one character of the six who lives in the country. She is earthy, with a suggestion of wildness, and is associated with motherhood throughout. As a child, school oppresses her nature-oriented sensibility, and she craves the outdoors: the fields, the woods and the elemental life of the seasons. Love and hate are the two points of the dial in her heart: she loves fiercely and she hates with equal intensity. She hates the infernal man-made labyrinth of London, and she flushes angrily at the soft overt femininity that Jinny easily exudes. As the six of them meet in London for lunch, Susan hides her "square-tipped finger-nails [...] under the table-cloth" (p. 91) in embarrassment at her ruggedness, her harshness. One of her earliest memories is her rage at Jinny kissing Louis – an overwhelming and instinctive envy at something half-understood. But

Susan is also the most loved of the six: beloved, we learn, by Bernard while he was at university, and also beloved by Percival.

LOUIS

Louis is the son of an Australian banker, and he is constantly, perilously aware of his precarious place in proceedings, on account of his New World heritage. He has a slight Australian accent, and his life becomes permanently tinged with the task of compensating for that fact. He is over-observant of English rituals and social traditions and full to the brim with respect for the world he means to enter as an initiate. His mind is fine and exact, in a way which Bernard hopelessly envies; he is perhaps the cleverest of them all, and yet he must shore up his place in the social fabric through labour. As a fellow outsider, Louis has a special connection with Rhoda, and the two embark on a relationship, although it does not last. If ungrounded within English society, Louis nonetheless has a rich, time-spanning sense of himself. He has a past-life memory of himself as a woman carrying a vase to the banks of the river Nile in Ancient Egypt, and it is this unfolding vision of history – with himself on the crest of the ever-advancing wave – which pushes him forward.

RHODA

Rhoda is the most peripheral of the six. She is quiet and self-effacing, but also raw, and permanently aware of her own marginality within the group. Not at ease and comfortable in her body like Jinny, nor endowed with the rough vitality of Susan, she is ghostlike and dwells at the side of things. In addition to her withdrawing tendencies, she is set apart from the other six by her almost mystical inner sight: she looks ahead, to the far distance, beyond the most extreme verge, and seems to be able to catch sight of something that eludes the others. Of the six, she is the only one to die in the novel. We learn in Bernard's final monologue, in an offhand way, that Rhoda has killed herself.

NEVILLE

Neville is forceful and neat, appreciating the good Roman order of his favourite Latin poets – in whose footsteps he follows, becoming a successful poet himself. He is also anti-authoritarian, despising the Church and the hypocrisy of the school chapel sermons. Neville sees divisions clearly and sharply, and in this way is the opposite of Bernard, who views himself as an extension or projection of others, and has nothing bad to say about anyone. Neville, who was in love with Percival, is the most deeply affected by his death in India.

JINNY

Jinny draws comfort and happiness from her body, and finds a sense of clarity and straight-forward truth in her sense of physicality. She can attract attention and conversation easily, and we get the impression that the night-life of London furnishes her with what she needs from life. She is a connoisseur of self-presentation, and all of the others – apart from Susan, who feels too nearly threatened by her – respect and appreciate this quality. Like Bernard, she is dependent on others for a great amount of her sense of self. And yet, like Bernard, we see her entering old age gracefully. Her bodily confidence is not a matter of vanity or superficial appearance, but a kind of corporeal ontology which grounds her in herself.

PERCIVAL

Percival is the only character with no voice in the novel. He goes through school, adolescence and young adulthood with the others, before going out to India and dying tragically in a fall from his horse. As his name suggests, Woolf gives him the aura of the chivalric English hero, and this quality is constantly noted by the others: "You have lost a leader whom you would have followed" (p. 116). His tragic death lends an air of decline to the dream of Englishness, while it also has a resonance with Geoffrey Chaucer's (English poet, c. 1343-1400) *The Canterbury Tales*: in 'The Knight's Tale', after winning the battle, Arcite is thrown from his horse and dies from his injuries.

ANALYSIS

TIME AND PHOTOGRAPHY

Virginia Woolf's earlier novel, *To the Lighthouse* (1927), features a very famous moment. The first section of the novel details Mr and Mrs Ramsay's stay at their summer home in Skye, surrounded by family and friends. We become settled in and at ease with the characters, with Mr and Mrs Ramsay and the children, and we certainly are not expecting what happens next. The following section, economically entitled 'Time Passes', zooms suddenly and fiercely out. We are now watching time passing. We see the house in Skye while the Ramsays are not there, and we learn obliquely of things that have happened out far beyond our view. It is almost like watching a sped-up time-lapse photograph or a fast-forwarded movie. Our viewpoint moves from the highly subjective, interior and charismatic thoughts of the characters, to the objective and the exterior – almost as if we were sharing in the perspective of time itself. When the Ramsays return in the third section of the novel, we find everything changed. Years have passed in only a dozen or so pages, yet they have taken a cruel tithe.

In *The Waves*, Woolf clearly wanted to replicate and extend the device which she employed in *To the Lighthouse*. We might think of each chapter-opening, each sinuously descriptive passage of the waves breaking on the shore, as a 'Time Passes' sequence in miniature. The vision of nature doing what it does every day of every month, year in year out, and has done from time immemorial, takes on a mythic grandeur; next to it, human months and years contract into fragments of seconds. Woolf's skill in the novel is to bring this objective evocation of time into communion with the human experience of it. We see it working; over the course of the novel we see Bernard and Susan and all the others grow from children into respectable adults. We see them change, but we also witness them becoming aware and reflecting on the nature of that change themselves.

Alongside the development of Modernism in literature, the early 20th century also saw the rapid development of photographic technology.

Although the photographic process had been around for a hundred years or so, it was only towards the tail end of the 19th century that this technology became more widely available, with Kodak releasing their easy-to-use cameras. Of course, these years also saw the development of the cinema. By 1917 a film industry had been established in Hollywood which over the next ten years would come to dominate the Western world. These vast new territories of culture and technology were of great interest to contemporary writers and thinkers. In 1935, Walter Benjamin (German-Jewish philosopher, 1892-1940) would publish his famous essay, 'The Work of Art in the Age of Mechanical Reproduction', which remains perhaps the most well-known and influential essay on art written in the 20th century. As a great artist and a tireless critic of modern culture, Virginia Woolf was not unaffected by these developments, as her essay, 'The Cinema' (1926) demonstrates.

The technologies of film and photography are at least superficially absent from *The Waves*. No character goes to the cinema. No-one has their photograph taken, nor keeps a snapshot on their mantelpiece. The influence of photography on the novel is deeper, and more subtle than this. For Modernist writers like Woolf, the significance of photography lay in its claim to objectivity. The camera, or camera-eye, replicated reality entirely mechanically. It seemed to offer a vision of the world as it is, unseen by human eyes – a world of the optical unconscious. The eye of the photographer might select the frame of the shot, but the actual photograph – the image itself – remained that seen by the camera lens. This concept proved radically influential for a whole generation of writers, who looked to the camera for a new model of what poetic representation might accomplish. In the United States, John Dos Passos' (American writer, 1896-1970) *U.S.A. Trilogy* (1930-1936) featured 'Camera-Eye' sections which picked up abstract and fleeting sensory impressions with the sheer clarity of a photographic lens.

Woolf's descriptive passages in *The Waves* function in the same way: they endeavour to represent the objective, elemental world that lies beyond human vision. No human figures occupy these sequences, or if they do, they are distant abstract forms which receive no more attention from the narrator's gaze than the clouds, the birds and the tree-branches. In this way, the photographic gaze takes on a timeless quality, or at least appears untouched by the passage of time.

WOOLF'S STREAM OF CONSCIOUSNESS

'Stream of consciousness' is probably the most well-known and most referenced stylistic device of Modernist fiction writers, and Virginia Woolf, alongside the likes of James Joyce (Irish writer, 1882-1941) and Marcel Proust (French writer, 1871-1922), is probably one of the most famous of its practitioners. Ask any literature student to describe Woolf's writing, and it is highly likely that they will at some point invoke the 'stream of consciousness' prose style. Coined by William James (American philosopher and psychologist, 1842-1910), 'stream of consciousness' refers to a writing style which attempts to recreate the unfolding processes of the human mind. Rather than simply narrating events or relaying feelings, it seeks to emulate a character's mental experience of thought and feeling. Recreating these exertions, the prose might well become labyrinthine, associative and discursive, and even disregard conventional punctuation.

The Waves, although its punctuation all remains intact, seems to fit the bill perfectly for this style of writing. Apart from the purely descriptive chapter-openings, the novel is made up entirely of deeply confessional and exploratory monologues. As each character takes it in turn to speak, we are surely witnessing the innermost workings of their minds. The vaults they perform between present and past, reality and memory, between the mundane every day and the hyper-poetic, are constantly arresting and engaging, and surely the stuff of 'stream of consciousness'.

However, considering the novel is called *The Waves*, and is based around this very particular movement of water, it might be worth reconsidering our understanding of Woolf's style in terms of the 'stream of consciousness'. For perhaps the very form of the novel and the nature of Woolf's writing reflect something of the action of waves, of the tide, pushing in and out again in a great recurring cycle, from one side of the world to another. A 'stream' is one-directional: water runs down and out, and though it replenishes at the source, it nonetheless goes only one way. But waves move in and out: they physically propel themselves forward, before surging back again, all the while moving up or down the beach as the tide moves in or out.

Taking this action as her central conceit, Woolf aims to portray a similar logic animating human experience. In this reading of the novel, the characters' soliloquies are not separate streams running in parallel, but are overlapping and interlocking waves, recycling and reclaiming imagery from each other, gaining substance and form from one another. In the final chapter, which is narrated entirely by Bernard, Bernard reflects: "I have been talking of Bernard, Neville, Jinny, Susan, Rhoda and Louis. Am I all of them? Am I one and distinct? I do not know" (p. 222). In a world which is formed of language, personal identity becomes amorphous. The clear distinctions we make between this and that, then and now, the self and the other, become suddenly less clear.

FURTHER REFLECTION

SOME QUESTIONS TO THINK ABOUT...

- Describe how Woolf conveys the effect of time passing in the novel.
- Find one reference to another work of literature in *The Waves* and consider why it occurs at that precise moment, and how it might be read against the wider action of the story.
- To what extent should we view any of the characters as extensions of Virginia Woolf herself?
- *The Waves* is renowned, along with other classics of high Modernism, as a difficult novel to read. With reference to a particular passage, try to describe the nature of this difficulty.
- *The Waves* is sometimes regarded as a kind of middle-ground between prose and poetry. Does it make more sense as one or the other?
- Poetic images occasionally recur through different characters' monologues. How might you explain this?

- Which character do you identify most with and why?
- We never hear Percival's voice in the novel, and yet he is a recurrent figure, presented to us repeatedly by the six characters. What effect does this silence have?
- Making stories is Bernard's life-long struggle. How might we read *The Waves* beside Bernard's own difficult and unfulfilled literary project?

We want to hear from you!
Leave a comment on your online library
and share your favourite books on social media!

FURTHER READING

REFERENCE EDITION

- Woolf, V. (2006) *The Waves*. London: Penguin.

MORE FROM BRIGHTSUMMARIES.COM

- Reading guide – *A Room of One's Own* by Virginia Woolf.

- Reading guide – *Mrs Dalloway* by Virginia Woolf.

- Reading guide – *Orlando: A Biography* by Virginia Woolf.

- Reading guide – *To the Lighthouse* by Virginia Woolf.

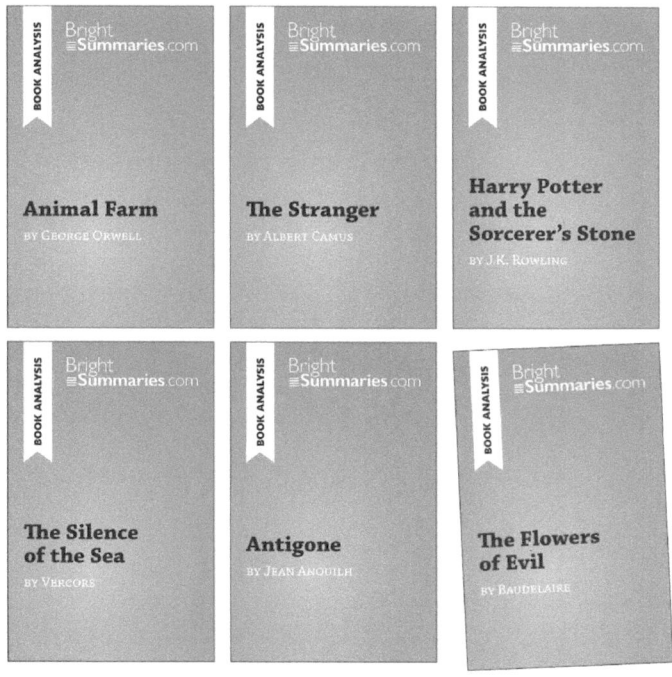

www.brightsummaries.com

Ebook EAN: 9782808017763

Paperback EAN: 9782808017770

Legal Deposit: D/2019/12603/55

Cover: © Primento

Digital conception by Primento, the digital partner of
publishers.